In
Meditation

In Meditation

Carroll Blair

Aveon Publishing Company

ISBN: 978-1-936430-40-6

Library of Congress Control Number
2011902861

Aveon Publishing Co.
P.O. Box 380739
Cambridge, MA 02238-0739 USA

Also by Carroll Blair

Grains of Thought
Facing the Circle
Reel to Real
Shifting Tides
Reaches
Out of Silence
Quarter Notes
By Rays of Light
Into the Inner Life
Gnosis of the Heart
Soul Reflections
Beneath and Beyond the Surface
Of Courage and Commitment
For Today and Tomorrow
Sightings Along the Journey
Through Desert's Fire
Offerings to Pilgrims
Human Natures
(Of Animal and Spiritual)
Atoms from the Suns of Solitude
Colors of Devotion
Voicings
Through the Shadows
As the World Winds Flow

1

*The motion of life is a circling
dance around the stillness
of eternity.*

2

What can bring you to truth,
to light, to bliss has always
been with you,
within you.

3

*You are made of what the
universe is made of, and more
than what it is made of.*

4

*No choice is there but to
live within the boundaries
of one's senses, but there are
other senses besides those
of the physical.*

5

The corporal of the earth is bound to the earth. The spiritual is of the universe, and beyond the universe.

6

*To absorb it all one cannot be
in the midst of it all.*

7

*A moment is a unit of time, but to be **in** the moment is to be in the infinite, which is outside of time.*

8

*To feel the full force of the
wind one must be still.*

9

Strength, grace, wisdom
are drawn from the peace of
inner silence.

10

Silence holds what needs to be said, and what needs to be felt that is beyond words.

11

In the sanctum of deep wonder
lies the heart of the sublime
leading to the sacred.

12

Earthly life is full of ifs,
but Life is only Is.

13

*They are always home
wherever they are who are
joined to the light within.*

14

*From deeper sensitivity
comes higher awareness.*

15

To be watchful is to be mindful.

16

The closer to truth the less adorned, the more naked it appears.

17

*Maturity of thought is present
when one can easily remove
oneself from the subject or
object of one's thought.*

18

*The higher question than
"Who am I?" is "What is this
that I am part of?"*

19

One hears many words but doesn't understand; another hears no words yet clearly understands.

20

*Every mind has its own
vocabulary of abstraction.*

21

*Many trap doors must one
go through in mind and spirit
to escape the trap of illusion.*

22

*As fog conceals the grandness
of the mountain, so illusion
conceals the grandness of life.*

23

*One is given only a blink
of an eye in cosmic time
to open one's eyes.*

24

Clearness of vision is preceded by clarity of thought.

25

What is always strong and true
cannot be seen nor sensed
by the undisciplined mind.

26

The sun lights for all seasons,
as does the light of truth
from the soul of light.

27

*As the arrow hasn't purpose
without the bow, so the
mind, without the soul.*

28

*In the absence of
awareness-cultivation, what
can be duly appreciated
or understood?*

29

*One acquires the
understanding
that one has earned.*

30

The best instruction is given by life, but demands an acuity of alertness to perceive its multiple signs in multiple forms.

31

*An open window must be
screened to take in the
freshness of the outside
without its dust and debris.
So too, a window of perception.*

32

*Passions can run deep,
but not as deep as the
dispassion of wisdom.*

33

To attach oneself to nothing
is to open one's inquiry into
the nature of all things.

34

*Objective thought is
integrity of thought.*

35

*To not look objectively at
what **is** is to never develop the
deftness of mind to sense
what could be.*

36

*The yearning for enlightenment
is beyond desire, and therefore
beyond the negatives that
accompany the longings
for what can never bring
true joy and fulfillment.*

37

What greater high can there be that sustains than the employment of the natural powers of mind and spirit?

38

*A single idea can take a
lifetime to reveal the
sum of its secrets.*

39

The communion with one's thoughts is a privacy of which no other should be more respected.

40

*One may hear a truth,
or read it on a page, or
have it explained in every
way, but its comprehension
can only come from
somewhere within.*

41

*What is of weight, depth,
profoundness must finally be
reached or discovered
on one's own.*

42

*One learns from observation
only if one brings learning
to the observation.*

43

*The wise think not of life
as merely for their pleasure,
but for their counsel.*

44

*Before engaging with the
depths of life there needs to be
a thorough engagement with
the growth of one's life.*

45

*To live with an increase of
consciousness requires an
increase of courage.*

46

*Time and again must
walls in the psyche
be broken if growth
is to continue.*

47

The growing mind is ever reconstructing itself around a spiritual center that remains.

48

*Living closely connected
to the unchanging yields
an instructive skill in
assessing the changes in
and around one's life.*

49

*It is never circumstance but
the response to circumstance
that determines the measure
of one's inner peace.*

50

*Unity with Life is not possible
when there is not unity within.*

51

*Folly allows passion to lead
the way; in the presence
of wisdom it is passion
that is led.*

52

*No more than hands can hold
water can one's happiness be
held in the hands of the world.*

53

*What is truly mastered
inside cannot be disturbed
or overcome by anything
from the outside.*

54

*Fulfillment is not a
search, but a creation.*

55

To grow gifts whose manifestations reach into the heights they must be rooted in as great a depth.

56

*The body needs space in
order to breathe, and also
the mind and spirit.*

57

Like a world without color
is human life without spirit.

58

*As fish to water, as birds to
the sky does the spiritual
join to silence.*

59

*Silence is a place [a space] like
no other, filled with power, wonder,
energy, creativity, pathways to
bliss unparalleled, inspiring
beauty and wisdom and love.*

60

*Light is before one and within
one, but to not be open to it
is as light shining on a closed
door of a darkened room. To
let the light into the room
[into oneself], the door
must be opened.*

61

What is for always is within you,
but it is as good as naught
when not being lived through.

62

Of the spiritual there is no compromise. One cannot "sort of" be living through the spiritual dimension of one's life.

63

*To mature in age is not
always to mature in wisdom.*

64

*The spiritual state is
an egoless state.*

65

*Until folly is faced
truth cannot be realized.*

66

*Before its blessings can
benefit a life the spirit
requires not only a clear
mind, but a clear heart.*

67

*There are forces of Nature that
nothing can destroy — this, like the
virtues that enrich and sustain life,
their compass ever pointing to the
ways of noble conduct as a guide
to living one's best.*

68

*One who is blind to the
graces of the heart sees
no wisdom, hears no wisdom,
knows no wisdom.*

69

*The heart is the key
to transformation.*

70

*The enlightened heart
expands with love; selfless,
giving, ready for all
wounds and healings.*

71

*To know the nature of
true joy one must know
the joy of giving.*

72

*Should one be less generous
with his or her light than
the sun is with its light?*

73

*The sight of goodness trying
to do its best is among the
world's most moving portraits.*

74

*During work of a noble
nature there is no need for
explanation. After work of
a noble nature there is
no need for explanation.*

75

*To move in love's direction
is to never go astray.*

76

*Compassion is the music of
humanity, directing the
rhythms and harmonies
of love.*

77

*Everything worth having
is in the life of giving.*

78

*The work of light inspires
a life to the fullness
of its power.*

79

*To live through the highest
power of one's life is to draw
from the power of Life.*

80

*True freedom is the gift
of the spiritual.*

81

*In the spiritual too, nothing is
automatic — gifts must also
be earned before they are given.*

82

*The higher ground is
in the depths.*

83

*The sacred can never be
embraced in an animal
state of being.*

84

Joy follows clear thought,
right engagement, right intent.

85

Great joy, great ecstasy
turns to responsibility — to
nourish and protect the
fruits of that ecstasy.

86

*Time to oneself is meaningless
objectively speaking if it
doesn't also lead to benefit
for someone or something
other than oneself.*

87

*When the spiritual is left out
nothing left in can function
with integrity and grace.*

88

*The spiritual is boundless, yet
has no place for baseness.*

89

*What is good from within needs
to get out; what is good from
without needs to get in.*

90

*The ego does its best to
enter the party of rejoicing when
growth has been achieved.
Paramount to further growth
is the negation of ego's entry.*

91

The endowments given to every life are meant to be realized in full, not to remain potential.

92

*Within the bounds of
humankind's limitations there are
endless possibilities of what
may be achieved.*

93

The very nature of Life is creative. How can that nature not also be part of you, who are a part of Life?

94

Gear for depth exploration,
not a life preserver has Life
placed before you.

95

*Gaining access to the
deepest depths of one's life
requires the same resolve
as drawing the sword
from the stone.*

96

*In the spiritual
something more for
you is something
more **from** you.*

97

*Quantum leaps may be
accomplished in spiritual
growth, but only when
preceded by quantum work.*

98

*The highest enlightenments
are not attained by a focus
of moments at a time, but
the focus of a lifetime.*

99

*For life to be a sacred
experience every moment of it
must be viewed as sacred.*

100

*The fruits of the earth
nourish the body; appreciation
for them nourishes the soul.*

101

*To be one with the universe
is to perceive the whole in
the one, and the one
in the universal.*

102

*Greater appreciation for the
unity of all is realized
with a greater appreciation
for their differences.*

103

To see only the humor of life is to see nothing. To see only the seriousness of life is to see nothing.

104

To be ever thinking is to be
ever growing in mind; to
be ever loving is to be ever
growing in heart; to be
ever humble in noble service
is to be ever growing in spirit.

105

*One's connection to Life,
its strength or its weakness
depends on where one is in
the journey of one's life.*

106

How far one has travelled is
not to be measured by how
long one has been alive.

107

*The journey of journeys is
that of the spiritual within.*

108

To play music well requires
a strong dedication. And so the same
with the music of one's life.

109

They are most confined
who are least disciplined.

110

*It is by virtue that the way is
found to higher virtue.*

111

*The true goods of a human life
are not purchased in the
marketplace, but harvested
in the inner gardens
of the spirit.*

112

*When ready to work
for the purpose of giving
one is ready to receive
of the spiritual.*

113

*The most purposeful lives are
those that bear fruit that
others may consume.*

114

*Love is the seed to
all that matters.*

115

*The noble life is to serve,
not to seek for others
to be of service.*

116

*Better than the world being
one's oyster is to be a
pearl for the world.*

117

*What is the prosperity
worth that is not of a
spiritual nature?*

118

To live well is to use one's gifts and talents for the good of life and others.

119

*Where there is honor,
honors need not exist.*

120

*What of the truly sublime would
care to be glorified — would not care
only to protect and project its light.*

121

*One's gratitude never
ceases once the divineness
of love is felt.*

122

*If the world were nothing but
pain there would still be reason
to love, to dance, to sing.*

123

*In the midst of inner suffering
the enlightened spirit can
still find peace.*

124

To be selfless is to be fearless.

125

The trembling spirit
cannot embrace.

126

*The great gift of life
cannot be realized until
it is fully accepted.*

127

*Their lives are most blessed
who look upon all in their lives
as blessing.*

128

To live in appreciation of every moment frees one from the need of placing a meaning onto life, living in wonder that it exists, that we exist, here and now, without explanation, partaking in the miracle-mystery, never ceasing in its power to amaze.

129

*Beyond the realm of knowing
is life's great mystery . . . one
can only be willing to embrace
it, to be part of it with
every atom of one's being.*

130

Darkness surrounds the sun,
but that doesn't prevent it
from shining.

131

*What speaks to one in his or
her life is waiting for him,
for her to speak back — in
creative expression.*

132

*What should be least silent
[most heard] is the spiritual
born out of silence.*

133

Never are they without
light who bring stillness
into their lives.

134

When the spirit is preparing to
arise, to become, it is being
emptied, accompanied by a
deep silence. When it is
becoming it is being filled,
accompanied by a
deeper silence.

135

*Through mind and heart the
spiritual finds expression,
rooted in the infinite.*

136

*One's life evolves so long as
one serves, so long as one loves.*

137

There are spiritual plateaus
that when reached inspire
the feeling that one has
been there all along.

138

There is always hope for the
individual to aspire to what
human life can be — to
experience its heights, its
depths, its ecstasies.

139

Not all wisdom comes from inside, but it all emanates from the inner journey.

140

*Guard the sanctity of your mind, your heart, your spirit as you would guard the sanctity of your life, for this **is** your life . . .*

and

141

Love . . . what else is there
to say   to give   to be

. . . .

ABOUT THE AUTHOR

Carroll Blair is an author of more than twenty books and the recipient of numerous awards. His work has been well endorsed and commendably reviewed. Among his titles cited for distinction are *Through the Shadows*, winner of the Pacific Book Awards, and *Quarter Notes*, winner of the Sharp Writ Book Awards. He is an alumnus of the Boston Conservatory and lives in Massachusetts.

www.ingramcontent.com/pod-product-compliance
Lightning Source LLC
Chambersburg PA
CBHW021154020426
42331CB00003B/58